Mary

THE PERFECT PRAYER PARTNER

Mary

THE PERFECT PRAYER PARTNER

FATHER KENNETH ROBERTS

Our Sunday Visitor Publishing Division
Our Sunday Visitor, Inc.
Huntington, Indiana 46750

Imprimatur
Monsignor Edward J. O'Donnell
Vicar General, Archdiocese of St. Louis

Copyright © 1983 PAX TAPES INC. Second printing 1985.

This edition © 1990 by Our Sunday Visitor Publishing Division, Our Sunday Visitor, Inc.

Our Sunday Visitor Publishing Division
Our Sunday Visitor, Inc.
200 Noll Plaza
Huntington, Indiana 46750

International Standard Book Number:
0-87973-451-5
Library of Congress Catalog Card Number:
89-64274

Cover design by Rebecca J. O'Brien

Printed in the United States of America

451

To John and Ann Ruskin, with love.

About the Cover

The Chi Rho, the symbol of Christ, comes from the M (Mary). She derives her dignity, honor, and strength from him, resting on his arm. As a perfect prayer partner, she leads into him.

About the Artwork

The Marian and Rosary artworks were created for this book by Michael Kenney, a famous St. Louis artist, who donated these sketches because of his devotion to Our Blessed Mother and in honor of his wife, Carmelita. Mr. Kenney's dedication and use of his talent to present Christ and his Mother are evidenced in these pictures.

I must add that Michael Kenney has painstakingly studied the Hebrew culture and the mode of dress worn by the Jews at the time of Christ, so that in these pictures, every detail is authentic.

All of the sketches are original and produced solely for this book and cannot be reproduced. Michael gives much of his time and talents to the Church; he is an ordained married deacon and is well known in Missouri as a leader in the Cursillo movement.

For your time, your talent, your inspiration, and your generosity in sharing your efforts with all of us, thank you, Michael.

Acknowledgments

Thank you, Michael Kenney, for your generosity in sharing your time, your talent, and your dedication with us in preparing this book.

Thank you, O.G. Waters Jr., for providing the photographs and for your patience and support throughout this project.

Thank you, Anna Marie Waters, for spending many hours listening to my tapes, recording my thoughts, and helping me piece it all together.

Table of Contents

Introduction

"Why do you want to write a book about Mary?" That was one of the comments I received when I told a few people about this endeavor. Here are a few of the others:

"That's fine . . . but will it sell?"

"Aren't there already a lot of books about Mary?"

"Will there be a lot of research?"

In response, let me state that the marketing possibility has not been a motivating factor, and yes, I am aware that there are many very fine books about Mary. And as far as the research involved, this is not a result of what information I have learned in my head . . . rather, it is a result of what I have gathered in my heart.

To those of you who already hold a special place for the Mother of God, I hope you will find this book a reinforcement of your attitudes and devotion, but for those of you who have not been aware of Mary's role in the Church, I hope it will provoke you to have a deeper understanding and esteem for her.

But these aren't the only reasons why I have written this book. I simply felt I must. . . .

PART ONE
MARY

Is It a Coincidence?

"Preach what you believe and believe what you preach." That bit of advice was given to me by an old priest shortly after I was ordained. I never had any difficulty following it until I found myself leading a tour to Fatima and Lourdes a few years ago.

Fatima and Lourdes were topics I had conveniently dodged, but that doesn't mean that I avoided talking about Mary. On the contrary, I emphasized her role in the Church, and intellectually I could accept that without any hesitation. But Fatima and Lourdes . . . that was something different.

As I sat on the tour bus gazing at the passing panorama, my mind went back to when I was a student in Portugal. That was a long time ago, over twenty-five years. That was before I was in the British Army Intelligence, before I flew with BOAC Air Lines, before my jet-set way of life, and before that stormy road that finally led me to the priesthood. How filled with zeal I was back in those days! I remembered how thrilled I was when I arrived at Fatima for the first time, how excited I was when I met the parents of Jacinta and Francisco; how enraptured I was when I knelt at the shrine, the place where Mary appeared; how I spent long hours writing to my mother sharing all these tremendous experiences, and how I accepted these miracles with unquestioning faith. This place which once had held so much marvel for me now provoked a different feeling within me, one I wasn't able to define. Why wasn't I the least bit excited this time?

The twelve people who accompanied me on this tour were aglow with anticipation and enthusiasm. I seemed to feel "left out." Why?

I tried to analyze my feelings. So much had happened to the Church since I was a twenty-one-year-old student in Portugal. For now I was a product of the post-Vatican II priesthood and didn't feel "comfortable" with Fatima or apparitions anywhere. In fact, I had discreetly swept it under the rug and neither rejected nor accepted it. Fatima seemed too right-wing, so I managed to preach all these years without referring to it.

My thoughts were interrupted by Michael, our tour guide, who handed me the microphone. "Father, I'm sure you can tell them more about the miracle of Fatima than I." The moment was here . . . it was as if Mary were forcing my hand.

I cleared my throat a little nervously and began on somewhat of a negative note. "First of all, let me explain that the Church does not force you to believe in Fatima. It merely states that they have investigated and there is nothing against faith, so Catholics may believe it if they choose. But let me assure you that you don't have to believe it to be a good Catholic." *(Why am I saying this to these people? They DO believe it or they wouldn't be*

14

here. *Perhaps, I'm trying to reassure myself. What do I believe?)*

"In 1911, an anti-religious government took over Portugal, persecuting both Church and nobility. The royal family of Portugal sought exile in England, and many priests and religious suffered imprisonment, rather similar to the persecution in Iron Curtain countries today. It was six years later, on May 13, 1917, at midday, when three little children, Lucy, Jacinta, and Francisco, saw a remarkable event in the Cova da Iria near Fatima. They were minding sheep when they claimed to see a beautiful lady appear above a tree."

As I continued the story, the group on the bus listened intently. It was toward the end of the account that I began to listen to my own words. "The lady continued to appear on successive months on the thirteenth. The children asked her, "Will we go to heaven?" and the lady replied that Jacinta and Francisco, the two youngest, would go to heaven very soon, but that the eldest, Lucy, would remain on earth to spread the message. This prophecy has been fulfilled; the two youngest died within a short time, and Lucy, a Carmelite nun, is still alive today, living in Coimbra. Was that a sign or a coincidence?" *Which was it? . . .* I asked myself.

"The children reported that a force of atheism would spread from Russia and persecute the Church worldwide. The last apparition at Fatima was accompanied by a dancing sun in the sky, and it was seen by thousands and thousands. The day was

15

October 13, 1917, and the Russian Revolution began that same October." *(Another sign or coincidence?)*

I finished my little narrative emphasizing that "the Church does not force you to believe or dissuade you from believing that what happened here is a miracle." I handed the microphone to Michael.

"I have some bad news for you. Because we were delayed in our departure from the hotel this morning, and due to the traffic, we will not arrive at the shrine early enough to say Mass. There is a regulation in Fatima that no Masses can be said after twelve noon, and we will not arrive before one o'clock. I'm very sorry."

Sighs of disappointment filled the bus.

"Can't they make an exception for foreign travelers?" one woman asked.

"No, I'm afraid not. They are very strict about their rules. I have never known them to make an exception. . . . I'm afraid to be granted permission to say Mass at this time of day WOULD TAKE A MIRACLE . . . no pun intended," he added.

"Well, if that's what it takes, then we'll just pray for one," was the response from another woman on the bus.

What faith! I thought as a trace of envy stabbed at me. I said a silent prayer and asked that I could experience just a bit of their childlike, unquestioning acceptance.

It was five minutes before one o'clock when we pulled up at the Shrine. Since it was only the beginning of May, the huge crowds were not present; only a few hundred people prayed silently close to the chapel that marked the spot where the apparitions had taken place.

I caught sight of a nun hurrying from the square, so I approached her. "Excuse me, Sister, do you know of a convent nearby where I can say Mass?" I asked in Portuguese.

"It is not possible to say Mass after twelve, Father. Don't you know the rules?" she answered abruptly.

"I know, Sister, but we're from the United States, and we had planned to arrive here in time for Mass today but were delayed in our departure from Lisbon. We're only here a few hours, Sister, and I still haven't said Mass today."

She smiled as if she understood our dilemma. "I'm curious, Father, why did you single me out from the many others?"

"I don't really know . . . you just caught my eye when I left the bus. Why do you ask, Sister?"

She thought for a moment, "You see, I'm the sacristan in charge of the Shrine. I'm going to break the rules and let you say Mass there. I believe God wants it."

I practically tripped over my own feet in my rush to share this news with my group. They were so excited about the fact that we could have Mass, but when I told them it would be said at the Shrine, they were downright overwhelmed . . . all except the woman who had made the statement about praying for a miracle. I said to her, "Wasn't that a stroke of luck? Out of all the people around the Shrine area, that nun caught my eye. Had I waited a minute longer she would have been gone. Here she turned out to be the one who was in charge of the Shrine altar. What a coincidence!''

She merely stated in a matter-of-fact voice, "No, Father, not a coincidence, a sign."

Sign or coincidence. These words kept ringing in my mind as I vested for Mass. I found myself being very confused, so I put it away, because the more I speculated about it, the more confused I became.

At one o'clock, I began Mass as the bell tower chimed the "*Ave.*" Along with my group, there was a young man who was also responding in English. Afterwards, I approached him. "You're an American."

Shaking my hand, he replied, "Yes, Father, I'm from New York. My name is Bob Neswich."

"Are you a tourist also?"

"Oh, no. I've lived in Fatima for seven years. I decided to dedicate my life to the canonization of Jacinta. I work in the religious-goods store in Fatima, and I attend Mass here every day at noon. But today, it's like a little miracle."

"Why?"

"Because today I was so engrossed in my work, crating a huge statue of Mary to be sent to California, that I lost track of time. It was 12:45 when I looked at my watch, and I couldn't believe it. I told Our Lady, 'Mary, how could you let me miss Mass today?' So I asked for a little miracle — I'm

18

certain this is it. In my seven years here I have never known a Mass to be said at 1:00 P.M.''

After a quick lunch, we went to the home of Jacinta and Francisco, where we met their older brother, John, who posed for photos with us. From there we headed for Lucy's home, where her sister, Maria dos Angelos, was sitting by the door. We toured the tiny house, so typical of poor Portuguese peasants, and then we took more pictures. Just as we were about to leave, Maria asked for my blessing and suggested that we go to Coimbra to see her sister, Lucy. Coimbra was two hundred miles north, and we were due to go south according to our tour plans. That meant quite a detour. ''Will we be able to see Lucy?'' I asked incredulously.

''No, but if you were granted permission to say Mass, she would see you from behind the grille.''

I was familiar with Coimbra, a beautiful university town, as famous to Portugal as Oxford and Cambridge are to England. And since Coimbra is one of the oldest universities in the world, I felt it would be an interesting experience for my group. When I discussed the possibility of altering our travel route, I was surprised at Michael's eagerness to accommodate us, because a two-hundred-mile detour from Lisbon was certainly out of our way.

It was 11:00 A.M. the next day when we arrived in Coimbra. My anxiety was mounting again about the possibility of saying Mass, for I wasn't sure what the rules about Mass after twelve would be in this area. Several times we had to stop and ask for directions to the convent. It was a few minutes before noon when we finally arrived at the place where Lucy lived.

The nun who greeted me didn't even give me an opportunity to ask about saying Mass; she immediately informed that it would be impossible. I asked her if she would take a note to Lucy for me. My message was a simple request to be remembered in her prayers. She told me to wait and she would return in a few moments. That ten-minute interim seemed an eternity because I knew my group, still sitting in the bus, would be waiting to hear whatever I had to tell them. I mentally prepared myself to give them the sad news that we would be unable to have Mass here. Finally, Sister returned, smiled, and reassured me that Lucy received my note. I thanked her for her courtesy and was about to leave when she stopped me. "Father, Reverend Mother requested that you say Mass in our community chapel. Lucy will be behind the grille."

Once again my little group applauded the good news and praised God for all the favors bestowed upon us. These people's faith was like a shot of adrenaline to my spiritual energy. There I was, "their leader," and my role was to lead them on a pilgrimage and share pertinent information about the places we visited. I was sharing with them all the things I had learned in my years of studying; they were sharing with me all the things they learned in their years of believing.

We were much blessed as we continued our tour through Spain. The number of little signs — or coincidences — increased, and it would take a whole book to tell you all about them. Some that were especially meaningful to me were offering Mass at the same altar as John of the Cross in the Carmelite chapel where St.Teresa of Ávila was superior and being invited to celebrate the main Mass for the pilgrims at the Shrine of Our Lady of the Pillar in Zaragoza, a rare privilege.

The last leg of our trip was Lourdes, and we charted our long journey to be there in time for the candlelight procession. Since I had visited Lourdes many times, I knew that there should be no restrictions about our group having a private Mass after the procession, so we relaxed and enjoyed the scenery. Michael asked me to take the microphone and brief everyone about the miracle of Lourdes. I complied, though I was certain this group knew as much about it as I did.

I no longer found it as difficult to relate as I did when we first started our trip. By now, I had become accustomed to these little coincidences that marked our way. However, I must admit that I was still somewhat in awe of the faith that my little group of pilgrims displayed as I overheard them exchanging stories about the miraculous cures that occurred in Lourdes. Still, I wasn't convinced that I would have the nerve (*or was it faith?*) to ever tell our little experiences to my fellow religious and attribute it to anything but coincidence. My intellectual pride was too inhibiting.

21

The candlelight procession was beginning to form as we, armed with candles and rosaries, searched for the United States representation and took our places. My thoughts wandered as I looked into the faces of the people passing around me, all colors, all nationalities. They all came here for a reason. I found myself imagining many of them suffering from some incurable malady and journeying here to beg Mary's intercession and be cured. I wondered how many would go away disillusioned. Their faith had brought them here, but would it be with them when they left this place? Would they still believe as strongly? I began to pray that they would return to their homes with their faith unmarred, and if possible, increased. (*But what about me? I had no incurable disease. I wasn't in need of a healing . . . or was I?*)

When the procession ended, we made our way to the Basilica to have our private Mass. "All the lights are out, Father. It looks like they've locked it up for the night."

"But they have always permitted Mass here at odd hours . . . I don't understand." I felt embarrassed because I had given this such a buildup when we were on the bus.

There were more sighs of disappointment. I tried to recover the moment. "Don't give up. Let me ask someone. . . ."

I saw a nun standing close to the great doors of the basilica. (*Here we go again. Could you work something out, Mary? One more time!*)

"Sister, where can I get permission to say Mass tonight?"

"Impossible, Father. No Masses after night prayers." She was very emphatic.

"But seven years ago when I was here I celebrated Mass, and it was close to midnight!" I explained.

"That was seven years ago, Father. It is no longer a practice."

I was persistent. "Is there someone here I could talk to? We don't have to say Mass right here. If I could just be granted permission to say Mass anywhere."

She pointed to a cleric in a long cassock whose back was toward me. "You might ask him. He's the brother in charge of the English-speaking groups."

I tapped him on the shoulder. "Excuse me, Brother." He wheeled around suddenly. I couldn't believe my eyes. "Brother Gregory!"

"September the fourteenth! What are you doing here?" He was as excited and amazed as I. It was unbelievable seeing Brother Gregory again after all these years. He had been my teacher at St. Mary's when I was in high school, and he never identified his students by name. Instead, he addressed them by their birth dates. It was his way of keeping his memory sharp, as a sort of a mental exercise. Apparently it was successful, for September the fourteenth is my birthday and he had remembered that although it had been over thirty years since he taught me. I never expected to see him again; he was a memory that I had tucked away fondly.

Needless to say, we had our Mass. Later, we sat together in the hotel lounge recapping the highlights of the day. I said to my friends, "I'm still amazed. After all these years, who would believe I would run into Brother Gregory and here at Lourdes, of all places? What a coincidence!" I bit my tongue; I knew that would get a response from someone. Just as I thought, the same lady who had corrected me in Fatima spoke up again. "No, Father, not a coincidence. It's a sign!"

That trip I made around ten years ago is probably one of the most beautiful I have ever made, certainly the most memorable. I too had received a healing at Lourdes. Not one as visible as if I had been able to throw away crutches or had been·cured of a physical malady, but it was, nevertheless, a healing. Until then, I had been suffering from intellectual pride and the fear of being criticized by my peers for preaching "pre-Vatican II spirituality." But at the end of that trip, I said, "Okay, Mary, you win. I'll preach your message . . . and that's a promise." A promise I'm keeping as I write this book.

All these signs and coincidences keep coming back to me whenever I'm tempted to rationalize extraordinary events or analyze every experience. A short time ago, I felt a renewed awareness of the validity of the Fatima messages when Pope John Paul II was shot in St. Peter's Square. Do you remember what date it was? May 13, 1981. Sixty four years to the day from when Mary first appeared

24

to the Fatima children. All these children testified to the fact that Our Blessed Mother spoke about the persecution of the Church, and Jacinta spoke of seeing a Pope weeping while the crowd outside mocked him.

Signs or coincidences? You must judge for yourself. But keep in mind, a sign is merely a coincidence . . . plus faith!

Her Name Was Mary

As I begin this book, I feel the urgent need to urge you to erase from your mind all of your former concepts of Mary and Marian devotion. Unfortunately, due to extremes of Marian devotions, images are often conjured up, and we visualize elaborate processions, blue-and-gold banners, and a rose-covered pallet where stands a plaster statue. The serene face of the statue, with its glass eyes, seems to gaze down at us almost as if it were waiting for a response. But how do you respond to a statue? You can judge it for its sculptor or its art form, but how can it really touch you unless you have become acquainted with the person whom this statue represents?

Concentrate on Mary, the person. Put aside, if you will, all the other titles lavished upon her — Star of the Sea, Refuge of Sinners, Queen of the Saints, Our Lady of Lourdes, Our Lady of Sorrows, Our Lady of Fatima, Our Lady of Guadalupe, Our Lady Help of Christians, The Immaculate Heart . . . and it goes on and on.

Think about the girl named Mary, the daughter of Anna and Joachim. See her as a young Jewish girl living in Nazareth, working with her mother, and going about the chores that belonged to the women in her village. She most likely lived in very poor surroundings all of her life, so the elaborate jeweled crown that artists have chosen to place upon her head would have been totally alien to her.

I'm trying to get you to see Mary as a young girl living according to the Mosaic Law, praying, working, and sharing with the people in her village the hope for Israel to be free.

She had feelings. She laughed, she cried, she felt pain, she felt depression, she felt fear. She knew sadness as well as joy. She was a REAL person, a REAL girl, a REAL woman, a REAL mother. She nursed her Baby, changed his diapers, wiped his nose, washed his clothes, fed him, played with him, corrected him, taught him how to count, taught him manners, taught him respect, taught him how to obey.

She listened to him cry for his milk, giggle, sing, and laugh out loud. She felt him feed at her breast, felt his soft breath on her cheek as he slept on her shoulder, felt his baby fingers wrap around her own, felt his arms hug at her neck, felt his lips touch her cheek. She watched him roll over for the first time, watched him crawl, watched him take his first steps, and watched him play with his friends.

As he grew, she saw his features change as he assumed some duties such as helping Joseph with his carpentry work. She probably applauded his first efforts to make something alone. Perhaps it was a box, a stool, or a simple toy to amuse himself.

Mary was a homemaker too. She washed clothes, baked bread, swept the floor, set the table. Picture in your mind Mary greeting Joseph and Jesus at the end of their working day. See the family at their meals sharing the village news.

When Jesus left home to begin his Father's work, can you see her hugging him, then waving good-bye, and probably saying a quiet prayer for his safety?

Mary is REAL, with real feelings like any other person, like any other woman, like any other mother. She doesn't reside on holy pictures, in shrines, on pedestals, in works of art, or in statues. These things are only reminders or symbols of her.

I hope that you will gain a deeper appreciation for Mary in these following pages and see her as God must have looked upon her . . . a woman filled with love and faith, doing what God asked her to do the best way she knew how.

Isn't that what he asks of us too?

Who Needs Mary?

Several years ago, I attended a prayer meeting with a few friends. One of the women in our group (we'll call her "Kate") had never experienced a Charismatic prayer gathering before, but she consented to accompany us after a mutual friend had told her of the healings she had witnessed. Since Kate had suffered from a very painful back ailment, which even multiple surgeries hadn't relieved, she finally agreed to go, but it was somewhat with "tongue in cheek."

I had never prayed with this particular group before, so it was a new experience for me also. Although it was an ecumenical group and the majority were non-Catholic, their prayer meetings were held in the basement of a Catholic church.

The scene was quite austere; the blank look of the cold, crypt-like wall was broken by a few antiques from pre-Vatican II days. There were a few old paint-chipped statues seemingly staring at us, a tarnished votive candle rack, and a tattered banner like the ones commonly carried in the days when processions were so popular. In the middle of the room, two rows of old wooden folding chairs had been placed to form a circle.

A dozen or so people were silently paging through their Bibles as we took our seats. After a few minutes, the moderator stood and called us to prayer, beginning with Scripture readings and then continuing with shared prayer. I was relieved to see

that the group was quite subdued, for I was aware
that Kate was very traditional and she would have
been turned off by anyone praying "in tongues."
But she was participating, and I had the impression
that she was quite relaxed.

The moderator asked if anyone present had a
special prayer petition. One of our group announced
Kate's back problem, then proceeded to go into
great detail about the surgeries, the long-term
therapy, the medication, and how ineffective all of it
had been.

Immediately the group stood while one
gentleman placed a chair in the middle of the circle
and directed Kate to sit. The relaxed expression left
her face as she took her place. No sooner had she sat
down than the whole group huddled around her for
the "laying on of hands."

I felt anxious for her and angry at myself,
because I hadn't thought to prepare her for this and I
knew this whole scene was totally unfamiliar to her.

Her relaxed expression surrendered to one of
confusion, perhaps even a trace of fear. She seemed
to be covered in "hands." Someone cried out,
"Lord Jesus, heal our sister!" Then, almost as if on
cue, voices filled the room in a language only
understood by God. The group was speaking in
tongues.

The rise of Kate's shoulders and her clenched
hands revealed that she was more than merely
uncomfortable. The moderator told her to close her
eyes and surrender to the healing power of the
Spirit. I watched her quickly span the faces around

her until she rested her eyes for a few seconds in the distance. While the group still chanted, her lips moved silently for a moment or so. Since my hand was on her shoulder, I could feel the tension leave as her body seemed to sink deeply in the chair.

I wasn't the only one who felt the relaxation come over her; the moderator called everyone to silence and in a jubilant voice cried out, "The Spirit has entered her!" My friend's eyes remained closed, and her lips continued to move silently in prayer.

"Give witness," the moderator directed as the crowd pulled back, watching her in anticipation.

"What?" Kate asked us she looked up with surprise.

"Give witness!" was the repeated command.

"I don't understand. . . ."

"Tell us what you experienced when the Spirit entered.

Still confused, she looked over the anxious faces, and in a very quiet tone, she began, "Well, this is all so new to me, this kind of prayer, and when everybody started making all those sounds and I felt your hands all over me, I got nervous and I really couldn't pray. But then I saw that old statue of Our Lady in the corner, so I asked Our Blessed Mother to . . ."

"YOU DON'T NEED MARY!" the moderator interrupted with a shout. She reached between the pages of her Bible, pulled out a picture of Christ, and thrust it at Kate. In a loud, determined voice, she said, "He is all you need. You don't need Mary!"

"God did," Kate answered quietly and simply.

A tense stillness hovered over the group for what felt like a very long time, until it was finally broken as Kate continued with remarkable calmness.

"You asked me what I experienced, but you didn't want to hear my answer. You see, whenever I find it difficult to pray, I ask Mary to pray with me. When I saw the statue in the corner of the room, I asked Our Blessed Mother to intercede to Jesus for me, to pray with me so that I could feel the peace of the Holy Spirit . . . and I did."

No one in the room could deny that Kate felt peace, because even after that unusual display of exaggerated zeal, Kate's voice, her face, her eyes, her whole manner remained peaceful.

After the prayer meeting, a woman took Kate's hand and said in a half whisper, "Thank you . . . your witness was beautiful. It reminded me of something I heard years ago, and I too, felt the Holy Spirit when I remembered it: TO JESUS THROUGH MARY."

Everyone was exchanging niceties as we were leaving except for the moderator, who was busy straightening the folding chairs and collecting song sheets. She still appeared to be irritated.

"Just a moment," Kate said as she walked away from our group and went toward the woman. I watched her say something, and then the woman stopped what she was doing and threw her arms around Kate in a really strong hug. The two of them stood there, hugging each other, not saying a word. Witnessing this reconciliation brought me an awesome awareness of peace.

We waited until we were all snug in the station wagon when, almost in unison, we asked, ''What did you say to her?''

''Well, it was really crazy, because I had no intention of saying anything to her . . . I didn't want to upset her any more than she already was, but when I reached in my coat pocket for my gloves, I pulled out this little bookmark along with them. I read the lettering on it and something compelled me to go over and share it with her. It was really strange . . . I just found myself going over to her and saying what I had just read on the bookmarker: JESUS, IN ME, LOVES YOU.''

So, what is the moral of this story? There are several, and I use it often to illustrate these main points.

Firstly, Kate was correct when she answered that God needed Mary, but he ''chose''to need her. He could have sent his Son to earth by just dropping him from the heavens in such a spectacular way that all the earth would have accepted him as the Son of God . . . but he didn't. Rather, he chose a young girl, filled with the love of God, to be the Mother of his Son, Jesus. And in her role as the Mother of Jesus, Mary has become a model of many virtues because she was a REAL person with REAL feelings, living a life of REAL faith and REAL trust in God.

Another point to be derived from this story is that Mary and the Holy Spirit are definitely compatible! Whether you're active in the Charismatic Renewal or a member of the Blue Army or Legion of Mary, keep in mind that Mary was very much in tune with the Holy Spirit. In fact, in the New Testament, Luke 1:35, the first person who received the Holy Spirit is Mary. "The Holy Spirit will come upon you and the power of the Most High will overshadow you. . . ." For this reason, I like to refer to Mary as "the first Charismatic."

Unfortunately, with some Christians, Mary has been a divisive factor, and she NEVER would have wanted that. Rather, I see her as a bridge uniting all Christians to Jesus. She was the tool with which God chose to put his Son on earth as a man. She bridged that gap between the human and the divine when she, as a human person, gave birth to the divine and human Son of God.

Our Blessed Mother's role has never been to take people away from Jesus. It has always been to bring us closer to him. The last words Mary spoke in Scripture give witness to her message. In John 2:5, she says, "Do whatever he tells you."

The last point I draw from Kate's story is that she felt compelled (I'm sure that was the Holy Spirit) to give that bookmark to the moderator, and it exemplifies one fact that as Christians we must always keep in mind: Whether you belong to the Charismatic Renewal, the Blue Army, the Legion of Mary, Marriage Encounter, Cursillo, whatever . . . we are all joined in the love of Jesus so we MUST have respect for one another's ways of reaching out to the Lord, even if it differs from our own. As the bookmark said, JESUS, IN ME, LOVES YOU.

Let It Be

I told you in the introduction that this is a "heart" book, not a "head" book. But if you want an intellectual reason for accepting Mary in a special role in the Church, read Genesis 3:15, about when God spoke to the serpent, "I will put emnity between you and the woman, and between your offspring and hers, He will strike at your head while you strike at his heel."

Every fundamentalist recognizes that the "offspring," the one who will strike at the serpent, is Jesus. Well, whose offspring was he? Who is his mother? Remember the Lord said, "her" offspring. Mary gave birth to Jesus, the one God said would strike at the serpent. So Mary definitely had a role in our redemption.

An interesting observation made by the great St. Augustine was that the first words of the angel when he came to Mary to tell her that she was chosen to be the mother of Jesus, and the first word of the prayer most identified with the blessed mother is "Hail" or in Latin, *AVE*. Reverse the spelling and *AVE* reads *EVA*, which is Latin for EVE. Now, reverse the roles: the first woman, Eve, got us in this mess, and Mary, a second Eve, gets us out of it.

Personally speaking, Mary has played a vital part in my private redemption by the fact that I am a priest. If you read my autobiography, you are aware that my mother had a great devotion to the Blessed Mother and you know too that she died just twelve days before I was to be ordained. It was a difficult cross for me to bear, and it brought with it many doubts about my vocation and the existence of a loving God. . . . I questioned everything.

After my mother's funeral, I left England and returned to Rome to go into retreat in preparation for ordination. I was bitter, and I had serious doubts that I should proceed with Holy Orders. How could I serve a God I wasn't sure of, or a God who could permit such a horrible thing to happen? My mother was to me as St. Monica was to St. Augustine . . . she constantly prayed for my salvation. For her to see her "wayward son" become a priest, I felt, was an affirmation of her life of faith and trust in God. Her prayers would be answered. For months she prepared for that great day when I would be ordained. She had a chalice engraved for me as an ordination gift, because she said that each time I used it at Mass, it would be a reminder to pray for her. And now, just twelve days from ordination, she was dead. She would never see me use that chalice she so dearly loved.

During that retreat, I was numb, full of doubts, bitterness, and indecision. I couldn't accept her death, and I was reluctant to turn my life over to a God who could be so "heartless" as to permit this to happen.

On the last day of my retreat, I sat alone in the very contemporary chapel. I couldn't pray. I found my eyes wandering over the modern sculptures and art. I wondered why they designed the chapel this way. It was so cold, void of color and form;

everything was so abstract, and I felt chilled by the surroundings. The only thing that broke the unfeeling scene was a vase of flowers put before a picture I couldn't identify. For days, I had looked at that picture trying to figure out what it meant, but I drew a blank: Now just one day before ordination, I was still staring at it (instead of praying), trying to figure out the symbolism. Then it hit me. It was the 25th of March, the feast of the Annunciation, the day we celebrate the angel Gabriel's coming to Mary. That abstract painting was Mary and the angel, but I still wasn't touched.

You see, I was to be one of the "new breed" of priests; I was in the first class ordained after Vatican II and I had taken a more sophisticated attitude. I learned my theology, memorized many texts, studied Scripture, and armed myself with as much as my head could hold to prepare me to go out into the world and spread the Good News.

But in the solitude of the chapel, I was alone with my feelings. Suddenly the numbness gave way to hurt, and like a little boy, I cried in pain. It was a breakthrough because my bitterness was like a dam holding back what I felt in my heart. "Why, God? Why did you take her now? What reason could you possibly have for robbing her of witnessing an event she had prayed for so many years? What kind of a God are you? Give me some answers!"

When I looked up, I dried my eyes and began to stare at the picture once again. It was as if the painting consumed me. I left the pew and stood before the picture to read the inscription, "*Fiat Mihi*

Secundum Verbum Tuum'' (''Be it done unto me according to thy word'').

That was my answer. Submission. Not only did I receive the answer in that hour, but it became my priestly motto: *FIAT*. Let it be. Not my will but thine be done . . . and Mary was the first to say those words.

By saying ''Yes'' to God, Mary became the model for all of us who are trying to put meaning to our lives, who want to pursue the road to sanctity, who reach out for strength in time of trial and suffering. Once Mary said ''Yes'' and permitted God's will to be done in her life, there began a chain of events that brought joy and sorrow — but in her faith and trust in God, she is an example for any human being experiencing almost any emotion.

In my own case, I couldn't make sense of my mother's death and it served as a source of doubt about my vocation, indeed, about the existence of a loving God. I had no peace until I repeated what Mary had said, ''Thy will be done.'' But when I finally said it in that chapel the day before my ordination, I felt a new commitment to God's will, and since that time, I have had to say it over and over when something I planned went wrong.

My God knows me very well . . . he knows my fickleness. I'm certain that is why he sent me another experience to remind me to say ''Let it be'' when I tend to get upset over things not going the way ''I'' planned. It happened on my ordination day. We were summoned by a messenger from the Vatican and told that the Holy Father, Pope Paul VI, would grant our class a private audience. We were ecstatic over that news, and perhaps somewhat amazed. A private audience with the Pope doesn't happen very often. What an ordination gift!

Pope Paul made a small speech, then he whispered something to an aide. To my astonishment, he came walking toward me. "Dear brother in Christ." He put his arms out to me. "I am sorry to hear of your dear mother's death. Christ surely must have a special task for you to give you such a cross to bear so early. I'll pray for your mother at Mass, tomorrow."

I stood there stunned. The Holy Father is going to pray for Mum! How pleased she would have been, and what an honor and endorsement for her quiet, persevering faith. I felt deeply touched and still shocked by the fact that he had been made aware of Mum's death. Then, almost as if I were nudged into looking up in a precise direction, my eyes rested on a beautiful tapestry. There it was again . . . the Annunciation, and the inscription, "Be it done unto me according to thy word." I'm sure that God wanted to make certain that I didn't forget that resolution I made to learn to live my priestly motto, "Let it be."

No matter what your circumstances may be, you too can model your life from Mary's in saying "Yes" to God, for no matter what life demands of you, it will be easier to handle if you submit to God with faith and trust. Hers was the prayer that brings peace.

"Let it be."

A Model for All Christians

Artists have depicted the Annunciation in many different ways; most often we get a picture of a beautiful young girl looking up at an angel with her arms outstretched as she appears to be in ecstasy. The text in the Scripture (Luke 1:26-38) gives a more realistic account. Mary was frightened. The angel said "Be not afraid, Mary." Also, we read that Mary was a very practical young woman, for she questioned how she was to bear a child when she was a virgin, "How can this be?" After the angel explained God's miracle to her, she said "Yes," but few of us realize what faith and trust were required of her to give that answer.

Mary, when left alone with her thoughts, probably had many questions, questions that any normal, concerned young girl would have. How could she tell Anna and Joachim, her parents? What would Joseph say? What would the villagers do when she could no longer keep her condition a secret? And would any of them believe her?

Mary's anxiety and fear had to be overwhelming ... she was human. Remember, in those days the punishment for adultery was death by stoning. Mary's worry was not just about shame or the fear of being misunderstood; rather, she had to fear for her very life. Saying "Yes" to God's plan was more than consent to be the mother of Jesus, it was an ultimate act of submission to his will with an ever-present trust that her God would protect her.

Still there were sorrows, but in these sorrows, Mary has become a model for all of us, a model from whom we can gain strength for whatever our situation may be.

For instance, has it ever occurred to you that Mary is a model for divorced people? "But she was never divorced," you might say. That is true,but she did experience an emotion that many divorced people experience. Rejection. In Matthew 1:19, we read that "Joseph had a mind to put her away" (in some translations these lines read "Joseph had a mind to divorce her"). She knew how it felt when someone whom she cared about turned away from her. She was promised to Joseph and now she was pregnant. Why would he NOT reject her? He knew that he was not the father of the child she was carrying.

You know, rejection is probably one of the most difficult emotions anyone can experience, and I hear it all the time when counseling. People come seeking consolation and advice in desperation, desperate because their spouses have told them the marriage is over and there is no longer any love. There is little I can say to relieve their grief; the hurt is so deep. Usually during this time, prayer is very difficult because the person, having experienced rejection, is burdened with doubt about the "fairness" of God. They don't feel they deserve this cross, especially if they have always been prayerful and faithful. Suddenly, their world is shattered when the one they love and trusted no longer loves them.

They don't trust anyone . . . sometimes, not even God.

I often feel that these people leave feeling somewhat frustrated, because occasionally they say, "Father, you just can't understand this feeling . . . you just don't know." But Mary knows . . . why not share some of the grief with her?

The Scriptures do not go into great detail, but a chain of events must have transpired for Joseph to hesitate about accepting Mary. During that interim, I'm certain she suffered the sorrow of rejection and the pain of being misunderstood. Finally, Joseph consented to take Mary as his wife (he too, is a model of extraordinary faith and trust).

If you have experienced rejection, Mary is the ideal prayer partner for you. She understands your pain and can intercede for you to make the pain easier to bear and hopefully to find peace again.

Mary is the model for unwed mothers too. Remember her marriage to Joseph came AFTER she had conceived, so she knew the pain of people whispering about her and the pain of having to tell her parents about her condition. She was pregnant with no husband, so didn't she wonder what her parents must think about her . . . what Joseph would think about her?

Mary loved the child she carried, and because she had faith in God, she accepted the suffering that came with it. Don't you feel that she often asked herself why such a joyful happening, the birth of the Messiah, could not have been easier? During her pregnancy, she had to travel many miles and then only to find that when the time came to deliver, she had no place but a stable. Certainly she would have chosen a more appropriate place for the Son of God to be born. The birth of her baby was not in an ideal setting.

If any of you reading this book are pregnant and not married, you can take Mary's example by saying "Yes" to God and bear the child in your womb rather than seek out abortion clinics, which are so very available in our society today. If you are single and already have a child, take her example and trust God to help you with your responsibility. And perhaps at times you feel alone; share your feelings with her. Mary knows. . . .

Mary is also a beautiful inspiration for the widowed because we can assume that Joseph died before Christ began his public life. Certainly, if he were alive, he would have been with her at the foot of the cross, and Scripture tells us (John 19:27) that the apostle John looked after her after the crucifixion. Imagine her loneliness, especially knowing that her Son was in so much danger. She did not have her spouse by her side to share this sorrow.

If you have lost your spouse, take consolation from Mary. She knew that pain too, and she endured untold suffering alone when she watched her Son give his life. Share your loneliness with her and ask her to pray with you for the strength to persevere. Mary kept the vision of eternal life before her; ask her to pray with you to acquire this too. Your separation is only temporary. Mary knows. . . .

Mary's role as the model of all parents didn't come to her just because she gave birth. She did all the things a mother does for her child. Did you ever consider that she experienced the generation gap too? Think about it. When Jesus was lost and she spent three days searching for him, then finally found him, he gave a somewhat flip answer, "Did you not know that I must be about my Father's business?" (Luke 2:49) or in today's language, "I've got to do my own thing!" If you are a parent of a teenager, I'm sure you've heard that line before.

Mary knew the worried feeling over a child leaving home and the concern for his safety. Take an example from her. Word probably drifted back to her from time to time about how her Son was stirring up the people along the countryside. She must have prayed hard for his protection, but ultimately she had to put him in God's hands . . . and trust.

Have you ever watched your child suffer? Mary did. She watched him be mocked, beaten, crowned with thorns, then NAILED to a cross. Perhaps you have sat by a hospital bed and felt that same helplessness of not being able to relieve your child's pain, or take away a disease or injury. Mary had that feeling, but the injury her Son endured was brought about by our sins. She knew the frustration of not being able to share the pain her Son was enduring and not being able to take it away.

Certainly Mary is the perfect model for anyone who has lost a child. She knew the suffering of watching her Son choke out his last breath. And when it was over, she held his lifeless body in her arms, that same body she had carried in her womb, rocked in her arms, and held on her knee. She knew the overwhelming sadness and untold sorrow of watching her Son's murder. Her faith in God gave her the strength to live through it and keep her vision focused on eternal life. She had to believe that her child went to a greater life. If you have lost a child, you must believe that too.

Throughout our lives, we experience sadness and disappointments . . . that's all a part of living. Often people turn toward their families for love and support to help them through their crisis. As a Catholic, you have two families, your natural family and the family of the Church. God, our Father, knows our needs. He gave us a big Brother, Jesus, to help us acquire eternal happiness through his teachings, then finally through his death and resurrection. God did not leave us spiritual orphans. At the foot of the cross stood Mary, not a statue, or an unfeeling hunk of stone, or pastels on canvas . . . but a woman who loves, a mother who cares. She completes the family of the Church. God, our Father, Jesus, our Brother, and Mary, our Mother. Jesus looked down from the cross and said, "There is your mother."

Why not call on her. She's a mother who cares, who understands, who loves. Mary knows. . . .

A Perfect Prayer Partner

A friend of mine tells the story of when she was in labor with her fifth child. It was in 1965 when many Catholics were still pretty confused about Vatican II, as most laymen still had not been educated as to what the Council was really telling us. It seems my friend was in the hospital, and as she puts it, "As my contractions became harder and longer, my "Hail Marys" became louder and faster." Her attending physician, a strong practicing Catholic, entered the room and saw her clutching her Rosary beads and praying quite loudly. He teased, "What's all this? Don't you know that the Rosary is out and Liturgy's in!"

"This is hardly the time or place for Liturgy, Doctor . . . and the Rosary is very much 'IN' for me!" She made her point quite clearly.

This story is a good illustration of how many Catholics really misunderstood the Church's stand on the Rosary and even the Blessed Mother too. Many believed that Holy Mother Church was dropping Mary and the Rosary. But tell me of anyone who made an official pronouncement in the Church that said Mary and the Rosary were out!

It amuses me that many fundamentalist Christians criticize us Catholics for including Mary in our prayer life, but they don't hesitate to ask their ministers to pray for them and they never hesitate to pray with one another. Many prayer groups have adopted the practice of having a prayer partner, a special person to share your prayers with, who promises to pray for you and with you. So, why can't Mary be a prayer partner? Who would have more "pull" with Jesus than his Mother?

There's proof of the power of her intercession at the Marriage Feast at Cana (John 2:1-11).

Mary went to her Son and told him about the problem — the hosts were running short of wine. He knew that she expected him to provide the solution, because he said to her, "My time has not yet come!" But Mary knew her boy. She went straight to the stewards and told them, "Do whatever he tells you." She didn't take "no" for an answer. At his Mother's request, Jesus worked his first recorded miracle. Now, that's whom I want pulling for me!

I personally can't understand why some people have difficulty including Mary in their prayer life. I think of it as praying with Mary, and Mary praying with me, to her Son . . . just as we do when we pray for each other. Could I find a more important person to pray with than the Mother of God?

Regarding the praying of the Rosary, I know that many Catholics have turned off because they see it only as "repeating all those prayers." If that's all there is to it, then I agree. It's boring, if you concentrate only on "saying" words, but the words are important because they are scriptural and they are used to time each meditation of the mystery.

Do you realize that for a thousand years the Rosary has been used by saints to contemplate the entire life of Jesus? Don't just think about the event each mystery portrays; experience it. Put yourself right where it's happening. Be a part of it.

The Rosary is a method of prayer in which a whole family can be joined, from the oldest member down to the youngest child. The scholar and the student, the saint and the sinner . . . each one can derive something from it separately as it is prayed in common. For centuries it was the only way for the masses, who could not read, to ponder Scripture and cover the essentials of the Christian faith. It was, and is still, a structure upon which to build a regular prayer life, for the mysteries, despite the passage of time, are an inexhaustible source for contemplation.

For each mystery meditated, one OUR FATHER, ten HAIL MARYs, and a GLORY BE are recited. This is called a decade of the Rosary. There are five decades to each set of mysteries.

In the Joyful Mysteries, feel the excitement of Mary when God becomes human flesh in her womb at the ANNUNCIATION. In the VISITATION, you are there with Mary and Elizabeth when they meet. At Bethlehem, be with the shepherds, see the Babe, see the star during the NATIVITY as Christ is born. Listen to the words of Simeon during the PRESENTATION. Then search with Mary for her Son and rejoice with her in FINDING JESUS IN THE TEMPLE.

During the Sorrowful Mysteries, feel the loneliness of Christ in the AGONY IN THE GARDEN. Hear his cries when he is SCOURGED AT THE PILLAR. See the blood come from his forehead as he is CROWNED WITH THORNS.

Watch him fall while CARRYING THE CROSS. Finally, be with Mary and John when the Lord Jesus gasps his last breath at the CRUCIFIXION.

And in the Glorious Mysteries, be present with the apostles and feel their excitement witnessing the RESURRECTION. Experience the mingling of joy and loneliness during the ASCENSION when Christ leaves them to wait for the COMING OF THE HOLY SPIRIT in the upper room with the apostles and Mary. Imagine the glory of Mary at the ASSUMPTION, when she was assumed, like her Son, into heaven, and crowned as the Queen of Heaven at her CORONATION.

Mary requested at Lourdes and Fatima that we pray the Rosary. It's the tool that for centuries has turned sinners into saints. But if you are among those who have packed away your Rosary beads in a jewelry box, or a drawer in a night stand, or a special place designated for sentimental trinkets, get out those beads! PRAY the Rosary with Christ's mother.

PART TWO
THE ROSARY

Three Ways to Pray

Now you are ready to meditate the mysteries of the Rosary. One way is just to look at the pictures and place yourself in the scene. Pick up your beads and say the first decade, looking all the while at the picture. You see, gazing at the picture is itself a prayer. In this way, you will come to understand why the Catholic Church has used all forms of art in decorating her churches. They were placed there not as mere ornaments but as aids to prayer. Stained-glass windows, mosaics, sculptures, and paintings — all of them are means by which we concentrate. Just as sunsets, mountains, waterfalls, and rivers swiftly running by lift up the mind and heart to God, their Creator, so too does art. For this reason, I have included artwork in this book on prayer, not to decorate but to inspire.

Another way to pray the Rosary is to meditate words that inspire. I would suggest, then, that you read the Scripture reference of each mystery. Read it slowly and let the words sink in, then close your eyes and be still as you say the decade.

And thirdly, you can turn the page and try to discover the feelings involved. If you experience the event in the slightest way, for a brief second, to the tiniest degree, God has really blessed you and you are beginning to really pray the Rosary in a special way.

The First
Joyful Mystery
The Annunciation
(Luke 1:38)

Mary's private prayer place is
quiet . . . comfortable . . . familiar.
It's the place where
she speaks to her God
and her God speaks to her.
Suddenly, a light fills the room
and an angel appears.
She's afraid.
HOW DID IT FEEL, MARY?
The angel tells her that she is
"Blessed among women"
and chosen to bear the Promised One.
Confused, but eager to do God's will,
she submits.
"Be it done unto me."
HOW DID IT FEEL, MARY?
From the moment she says
"Yes" to God,
she is changed.
The world is changed.
Soon she will know the pain of being
misunderstood,
misjudged,
doubted,
by the people she loves.
HOW DID IT FEEL, MARY?
But in the stillness,
alone with her God,
she feels the warmth of his love
in the miraculous Presence
growing inside her.
He's the Messiah,

the King of Kings,
the Son of God.
Yet to Mary, a humble girl,
he is her tiny baby.
She caresses him in her heart
until she can cradle him in her arms.
HOW DID IT FEEL, MARY?

Have you ever felt God was asking
something from you?
Something almost impossible to bear?
MARY KNEW THAT FEELING.
Did you surrender to God's will?
Do you ever suffer the feeling of being
misunderstood, misjudged, doubted,
still trusting that God will see you
through?
MARY DID.

The Second Joyful Mystery

The Visitation
(Luke 1:42)

Elizabeth is having a baby.
Being past childbearing age,
she will need someone to help her.
Unselfishly, Mary travels
to be with her cousin.
The journey is tiring and long
for this young pregnant girl.
HOW DID IT FEEL, MARY?
Perhaps, Mary feels that
she needs Elizabeth too.
Someone who will understand.
Someone to share her feelings.
When the two women meet,
instantly Mary knows that
Elizabeth is aware of Mary's
special secret.
"Blessed is the fruit of thy womb."
HOW DID IT FEEL, MARY?
Her miracle is recognized,
and Mary feels an overwhelming joy,
so immense that she cries out
in praise of her God:
"My soul magnifies the Lord,
and my spirit rejoices in God, my Savior."
HOW DID IT FEEL, MARY?
In the days that follow,
the expectant mothers share
their thoughts and feelings
about their unborn babies.
What color eyes?
What color hair?
But Mary has secret imaginings

that only the Mother of God can know.
HOW DID IT FEEL, MARY?

Have you ever felt a need
to share something with someone?
Didn't you feel joy knowing
that someone understood?
MARY KNEW THAT FEELING.
Did you ever feel the Lord so present
within you that you wanted to sing out
in love and praise of God?
MARY DID.

The Third
Joyful Mystery
The Nativity
(Luke 2:7)

Mary knows that time
is running out.
She prays harder,
and her anxiety grows
as each time she and Joseph
are refused a place to stay.
Doesn't anyone care?
. Her baby is ready to be born . . .
but where?
HOW DID IT FEEL, MARY?
Finally, they are permitted
the use of a simple stable.
Hardly the place she had imagined
for the birth of her Son.
No fine linens,
no crib,
no friends gathered around to help.
She and Joseph are alone,
and her time has come.
HOW DID IT FEEL, MARY?
Worry gives way to
acceptance,
as the young man and woman
wait out those final hours.
Joseph wants to do more,
but he does what he can.
Mary knows. She understands.
HOW DID IT FEEL, MARY?
Joseph tenderly and with quiet strength
attends Mary's delivery.
Then she lies there
in a humble bed of straw with

Joseph by her side and waits.
Soon Mary hears the Baby's cry,
and for the first time,
she holds her tiny Son
in her arms.
HOW DID IT FEEL, MARY?

Have you ever prayed for a special favor
and in your mind pictured
how great it would be?
Then something goes wrong?
MARY KNEW THAT FEELING.
Did you ever wonder why God
didn't answer your prayer?
Were you able to forget your own wants
and turn everything over to him?
MARY DID.

The Fourth Joyful Mystery

The Presentation
(Luke 2:28)

It's a big day!
The young couple are preparing
to take their Baby to the temple
according to the Mosaic law.
They are proud of the little one
as onlookers approach them
and smile at their Son.
HOW DID IT FEEL, MARY?
An old man meets the pair.
His eyes glazed with
wisdom and holiness,
he looks at the tiny Baby.
Simeon sees the WORD REVEALED.
Salvation wrapped in an infant's clothes.
Now Simeon is ready to meet his God.
HOW DID IT FEEL, MARY?
The happiness in the
young mother's heart is shattered
when Simeon looks
deep into her soul.
All the sorrow,
the suffering,
the sadness
which will be hers
is foretold by this holy man.
"And thy own soul a sword shall pierce"
(Luke 2:35).
HOW DID IT FEEL, MARY?
Mary looks at the Child
sleeping peacefully.
All her joy,
All her pain

is now cradled in her arms.
What suffering must
her Son endure?
She loves him so!
HOW DID IT FEEL, MARY?

How would you feel if
someone told you that
God planned to send
much suffering to you?
Wouldn't you wonder what
that suffering would be?
MARY KNEW THE FEELING.
Can you put your anxiety and fear aside
and accept from God's hands whatever
he has in store for you
with total trust in him?
MARY DID.

The Fifth
Joyful Mystery
The Finding in the Temple
(Luke 2:46)

Jesus is twelve now,
and he is lost.
Mary and Joseph search frantically ,
looking everywhere.
~~What evil has befallen him?~~
Is he sick?
Is he hurt?
Is he frightened?
HOW DID IT FEEL, MARY?
Where can he be?
The couple enter the temple
to seek consolation,
to pray for their boy's safe return.
What weight is lifted from them
when they see Jesus standing there!
What joy fills their hearts!
HOW DID IT FEEL, MARY?
Surely Jesus must know
how his mother would worry . . . .
Surely he would throw his arms around her.
Surely he would explain his absence.
Surely he would comfort her.
Instead, he merely asks,
"Didn't you know I must be about my father's
business?"
HOW DID IT FEEL, MARY?
Deep inside, Mary knows that
soon the day will come
when she must let him go
to do what he was born to do.
For now, he will go back
And be "subject to them" (Luke 2:51),

but just for a time . . . .
HOW DID IT FEEL, MARY?

Have you ever experienced the generation gap?
If you're the child,
do you feel that your parents don't
understand?
And if you're the parent,
do you feel that your child doesn't
understand?
MARY KNEW THAT FEELING.
Have you ever felt the joy
of being reunited with someone
whom you love?
MARY DID.

The First
Sorrowful Mystery
The Agony in the Garden
Mark 14:35

Pain is always difficult to bear
but even harder when you're alone.
Jesus needs his dearest friends
to be with him,
to give him consolation,
to ease the fear.
"My soul is sad even unto death;
wait and watch with me" (Matthew 26:38).
Instead, they fall asleep.
HOW DID IT FEEL, JESUS?
He begs,
"Father, if you are willing,
remove this cup from me."
He visualizes the torture
yet to come,
and the only sounds
he can hear are
the indifferent, rhythmic breathing
of his sleeping friends.
HOW DID IT FEEL, JESUS?
Soon he will be turned over
to his executioners.
A kiss will betray him.
A sign of love becomes
a sign of betrayal.
"With that, all deserted him and fled" (Mark
14:50).
HOW DID IT FEEL, JESUS?
Jesus is led away
To begin his human sacrifice.
To give his human life
for our eternal life.

"You will see that the Son of Man
is to be handed over to the
clutches of evil men" (Mark 14:41).

Have you ever felt betrayed
by dear friends?
Did you ever feel they
were indifferent to your pain . . .
that even God would not release
you from your suffering?
JESUS KNEW THAT FEELING.
Are you able to submit all
your fears, anxieties, loneliness
to God,
knowing that no pain is wasted
 when offered to him?
JESUS DID.

The Second
Sorrowful Mystery
The Scourging at the Pillar
(Mark 15:15)

Pilate gives the crowd
a choice,
the death of Jesus
or the death of a criminal.
~~Christ gave them love;~~
they give him contempt
as he listens to the crowd
clamor for his death.
HOW DID IT FEEL, JESUS?
He is tied to a post.
Now there is no escaping
the pain of each stroke
of the whip,
no escaping the insults
that cut as deeply as
the tears in his skin
while they continue to scourge him
and make fun of him.
HOW DID IT FEEL, JESUS?
Christ healed the sick,
raised the dead,
fed the hungry,
but he makes no move
to defend himself from
these evil men.
"This is why I was born
and why I have come into the world" (John
18:37)
HOW DID IT FEEL, JESUS?
His flesh is torn.
His sweat burns at each
mark of the whip.

"Like a lamb led to slaughter . . .
he submitted" (Isaiah 53:7).
"Oppressed and condemned,
he was taken away . . .
a man of suffering" (Isaiah 53:8, 3).
HOW DID IT FEEL, JESUS?

Have you ever tried to help someone
only to have your efforts returned
with contempt?
Did you ever feel a mental anguish
greater than any physical pain?
JESUS KNEW THAT FEELING.
Can you endure insult
knowing that you don't deserve it?
Can you rid yourself of
feelings of revenge?
JESUS DID.

The Third
Sorrowful Mystery
The Crowning with Thorns
(Mark 15:17)

The laughing crowd
grows louder
when they strip Jesus.
He stands before them,
his bare flesh torn
from the beating.
He is naked.
HOW DID IT FEEL, JESUS?
Now they cover him
with a purple robe,
a mocking symbol of
his kingship.
This crowd,
how they are laughing,
"Hail, King of the Jews!" (Matthew 27:29).
HOW DID IT FEEL, JESUS?
Every king must have a crown,
so Jesus receives his.
A crown of thorns
is placed on his head.
and pressed deeply into
His scalp and forehead.
His face tightens in pain
as the crowd continues to
mock the King.
HOW DID IT FEEL, JESUS?
What more satisfaction
can Christ give this crowd?
What more humiliation
do they want him to suffer?
But still they aren't finished.
"And they spat on him

and took the reed and
kept striking him on the head'' (Matthew 27:30).

HOW DID IT FEEL, JESUS?

Have you ever felt the hurt
of someone making fun of you?
Have you known what it's like
to be mocked and ridiculed
unjustly?
JESUS KNEW THAT FEELING.
Did you ever feel others
wouldn't be satisfied until
they broke you down?
Could you forgive someone
even after you were humilated?
JESUS DID.

The Fourth Sorrowful Mystery
The Carrying of the Cross
(John 19:17)

The splintered, heavy cross
digs deep into the already
lacerated flesh of Jesus' back.
Though weak, he forces himself
to lift the cross
and begin his walk to Golgotha.
HOW DID IT FEEL, JESUS?
The soldiers push back the mocking crowd
to make a path for Jesus.
His arms are aching.
His legs hardly support him.
His back tightens from the weight of the cross.
Each step brings a pain
that shoots throughout his whole body.
HOW DID IT FEEL, JESUS?
It's so hard to breathe.
He's dizzy.
The crowd seems to be swimming before his
eyes.
The thorns,
how they ache his head.
He falls,
but the soldiers demand
that he go on,
to drag His cross even further.
HOW DID IT FEEL, JESUS?
His vision is clouded by blood and sweat
dripping from his forehead.
He blinks and squints
to see a figure that he recognizes.
It's a woman with arms
outstretched to him.

She is crying.
She wants to be with him.
She feels his pain.
He sees his mother.
HOW DID IT FEEL, JESUS?

Have you ever had a difficult
cross to bear?
Did you feel that you would break
under the weight of it,
that you didn't have the strength
to go on?
JESUS KNEW THAT FEELING.
Can you accept the little crosses
sent to you each day?
Do you really believe that
God will help you bear them?
JESUS DID.

The Fifth
Sorrowful Mystery
The Crucifixion
(Luke 23:33)

Mary watches her Son's
large, callused hands being
laid on the wood.
The hammer drives
the huge nail through his flesh.
Jesus cries out in pain.
Now, the nails are driven
through his feet.
Again, he cries in pain.
HOW DID IT FEEL, JESUS?
Then the cross is lifted.
The weight of his body
tears the flesh from the nails even more.
Jesus gasps in agony.
In untold pain,
he looks down on those
who have not deserted him:
His mother, beloved John, and a few women.
Where are the others?
HOW DID IT FEEL, JESUS?
Three long hours
he hangs there,
naked,
battered,
mocked,
his blood draining from
his head, his hands, his feet.
Desperately, he calls to his Father,
"My God, my God,
why hast thou forsaken me?"
His throat burning and parched
He makes one final sigh,

"It is finished."
The human sacrifice is over.
The murder of Jesus is complete.
Christ is dead on the cross.
JESUS FEELS NO MORE.

Can you be indifferent to
the death of Jesus Christ?
Can you look at a crucifix
and not recall the agony
suffered for you,
JUST for you?

The First
Glorious Mystery
The Resurrection
(Mark 16:6)

It's early morning.
A woman cries at an empty tomb.
A stranger in white approaches her
as she pleads,
"Where have you put him?"
One word, and all is changed.
"Mary!" he replies.
She knows it is he.
HOW DID IT FEEL?
Peter and John run to the tomb
and look inside, only to find
the cloths where the body should be.
They tell the others in the upper room
who wait.
HOW DID IT FEEL?
In the locked room,
Jesus stands before his apostles.
The ten of them
renew their faith in their Savior.
HOW DID IT FEEL?
They tell Thomas
but he doesn't believe.
"Unless I can put my fingers
in the nailprints. . ." (John 20:25).
Jesus comes back again.
"Give me your hand, Thomas" (John 20:27).
Thomas believes.
HOW DID IT FEEL?
Jesus fulfills his promise.
The apostles know that
Christ has died.
Christ has risen.

Christ will come again.
HOW DID IT FEEL?

Have you ever felt
your faith faltering?
Have you ever wondered
if all that you believe
is true?
THE EARLY CHRISTIANS KNEW THAT
FEELING.
Perhaps Christ will call your name
and you will hear it in your heart
and know that he is with you.
You will feel joy and believe again.
THE EARLY CHRISTIANS DID.

The Second Glorious Mystery

The Ascension
(Mark 16:19)

There is something special
about this climb,
but what?
"A small circle of men
stands to pray,
and Jesus blesses them" (see Matthew 28).
His message seems so final.
They are happy, yet sad.
HOW DID IT FEEL?
He commissions them
to preach and baptize,
to take his message across the world.
He assures them of His presence
till the end of time.
There is something different
in his voice
and something special
in this moment.
HOW DID IT FEEL?
He raises his arms in prayer,
and then he is gone.
Nothing but a cloud
is seen
as they just stand there,
bewildered.
HOW DID IT FEEL?
"As you have seen him go,
so he will return" (Acts. 1:11).
Go back and do what you must do.
The apostles know
what that is,
but they must

pray for courage.
HOW DID IT FEEL?

Can you remember a time in your life
when you had to say good-bye
to someone you loved?
It was sad to see them leave,
but you had to go on
with a new phase in your life.
THE EARLY CHRISTIANS KNEW THAT
FEELING.
Did you go on your way
praying that God would guide you?
THE EARLY CHRISTIANS DID.

The Third
Glorious Mystery
The Descent of the Holy Spirit
(Acts 2:4)

For days they sat
all cooped up in the upper room.
They believed now and prayed a lot,
but still the power to do
what they must
was missing.
All they could do was wait.
HOW DID IT FEEL?
Suddenly a driving force,
an inner peace,
a love,
a courage
dispelled all fears.
They were all afire,
burning with new knowledge.
They felt the power.
HOW DID IT FEEL?
They left the room
and were amazed at
what they saw.
Their words were not their own
but his,
and thousands listened.
The world began to change.
This was the birthday of the Church.
This was Pentecost.
HOW DID IT FEEL?
Is something holding you back,
keeping you from doing the work
that God is calling you to do?
Do you feel the
lack of strength to do it?

THE EARLY CHRISTIANS KNEW THAT FEELING.

Can you call upon the Holy Spirit
to help you?
To give you the grace
to follow Christ
and spread his word?
THE EARLY CHRISTIANS DID.

The Fourth Glorious Mystery

The Assumption of the Blessed Virgin Mary
(Revelation 12)

Mary is lifted
from the earth.
What is this place,
so glorious?
It is the kingdom of God.
Trumpets blast,
and angels sing
a welcome.
HOW DID IT FEEL?
Jesus stands
with his arms extended
to meet her.
He looks so beautiful,
so radiant as
Mary rushes to him
for a fond embrace.
Was there ever
such a reunion?
HOW DID IT FEEL?
On earth,
among the followers of Christ,
there is a void
in the hearts of
those who knew her,
especially one
called John.
HOW DID IT FEEL?
She is the first of many
to join her Son.
Being without sin,
she is spared the corruption
of the body.

We, too,
each in turn,
will rise and be united
in body glorified.
HOW DID IT FEEL?

What kind of body
do you think you will have?
Your body has changed so often —
infant, child, adult, aged.
Who would recognize the baby in the man?
The final change is yet to come.
Think of how it will be.
THE EARLY CHRISTIANS DID.

The Fifth Glorious Mystery

The Crowning of the Blessed Virgin Mary (Revelation 12)

And a great sign
appeared in the heavens.
"A woman clothed with the sun" (Revelation
12:1).
No banquet,
no inaugural ball
was ever more resplendent.
The woman takes her place
beside her Son.
HOW DID IT FEEL?
"And the moon
was under her feet. . ." (Revelation 12:1).
Her work is done.
She awaits her award.
No woman was ever so honored.
HOW DID IT FEEL?
"And upon her head
a crown of twelve stars" (Revelation 12:1).
The moment has come,
and she is crowned
the First Lady,
the Queen of Heaven.
HOW DID IT FEEL?

Think of your last day on earth.
How will it be?
Think of your first day in paradise.
It will last forever.
Think of the reward
that Christ has promised you.
An eternity of happiness.
Do you know how it will be

after you die?
Close your eyes
and try to imagine it.
THE EARLY CHRISTIANS DID.

Mary and the Eucharist

I just could not write about Mary without sharing this with you.

In Luke 2:7, we read that Mary gave birth to Jesus "and laid him in a manger...." Do you suppose that was a coincidence?

We have become so accustomed to hearing the word "manger" used only in reference to Jesus' first crib that we often forget what a manger really is. A manger is an eating trough, a vessel which contains feed, a place to hold nourishment. Was it not prophetic that Jesus was put in an eating vessel from his very first moment on earth?

In John 6:51, we read Jesus' own words: "I myself am the living bread / come down from heaven. / If anyone eats this bread / he shall live forever; / the bread I will give / is my flesh, for the life of the world."

Read the rest of John 6 and discover that many disciples could not believe what they heard Jesus saying. "Many of his disciples broke away and would not remain in his company any longer." The fact I want to bring to your attention is that Jesus didn't call them back to explain. He didn't take back what he said. In fact, he turned to his remaining disciples and asked, "Will you also leave me?"

At the consecration of the Mass, the priest repeats Jesus' own words, "This is my body..." (Luke 22:19). We Catholics believe that at the moment these words are spoken, Jesus is truly present, body and blood.

This has always been a major point where we differ from our Protestant brothers. They believe that it is a symbol, and many of them, who reject the real presence of Christ in the Eucharist, also object to our devotion to Mary.

Mary ''laid him in a manger'' . . . a vessel that contains nourishment.

''I Am the Living Bread'' . . . that spiritual nourishment is now contained in another vessel . . . the chalice.

Ponder, too, that the first person to say ''This is my body . . . this is my blood'' was Mary. She said it before any priest; she said it even before Jesus did as she felt the Child kick in her womb. She said it too as she held the dead Christ in her outstretched arms. Yes, Mary was the first to receive the body and blood of Christ.

Epilogue

Thank you for the time you have taken to read this book. I pray that you have gained some new insights regarding Mary and her role in the Church. For me, it's been a joy to write. I suppose it's pretty much like someone who wants to share something very special with others . . . and Mary is very special to me.

If you have enjoyed the Rosary meditations, I would suggest that you obtain some of the very excellent literature available on the scriptural Rosary.* Also, if you would like to learn more about the recorded apparitions of Mary, there are many fine books available to you.**

For those of you who had already included Mary as your prayer partner, I have enjoyed sharing with you some of my thoughts and feelings about our mutual friend.

And for those of you who have never considered Mary in a personal way, this book has served as merely an introduction . . . it's up to you to get to know her better.

*See *THE SEVEN-DAY SCRIPTURAL ROSARY* by Larry London, available in book or audiocassette tapes from Our Sunday Visitor, Inc., Huntington, IN 46750.

**For example, *THOSE WHO SAW HER* by Catherine Odell, also available in book or audiocassette tapes from Our Sunday Visitor, Inc.

About the Author . . .

English-born Father Kenneth J. Roberts presently resides in St. Louis, Missouri, but his unique apostolate takes him all over the United States. He has appeared on over 300 radio and television shows and has earned the reputation of being one of the most powerful preachers in the Catholic Church today. His dynamic personality in the pulpit carries over to his writings as he constantly stresses the positive truths of OUR CATHOLIC FAITH and urges people to look to Christ and his Church for peace and fulfillment. Father Roberts' appeal is to all ages.

Also by Father Roberts:
PRAY IT AGAIN, SAM!

A beautiful book that combines just the right
amount of wit, instruction, and inspiration to create a
truly delightful reading experience. It appeals to all
ages and will be treasured by anyone seeking
spiritual growth. Father Roberts explains various
"ways to pray" with emphasis on the PRAYER OF
LISTENING. He refers to the Old Testament and
the book of Samuel. Samuel didn't recognize when
the Lord was speaking to him. . . . Do you?

AUDIO AND VIDEO CASSETTES ALSO
AVAILABLE:
Father Roberts teaches a complete course on the
beliefs and practices of the Catholic Church in an
easy-to-understand language. He answers many of
the questions mostly asked of Catholics about their
faith.
Other topics are also available.

For more information, write to:
Pax Tapes, Inc.
P.O. Box 1059
Florissant, Missouri 63031

OTHER BOOKS BY FATHER ROBERTS:
PLAYBOY TO PRIEST
In his autobiography, Father Roberts tells of his
unique road to the priesthood. Prior to ordination at

age 35, Father was a part of the jet set, traveling through Europe and the Far and Middle East. His adventures even included entanglement with a gold-smuggling operation. This book is both entertaining and inspirational as he describes his journey to the priesthood.

YOU BETTER BELIEVE IT

The popular catechism offers answers to youth in their own language, about God, the teachings of the Church, and about themselves. It has been heralded by parents and religious educators as well as young people themselves.

The above books may be ordered through:
Our Sunday Visitor Publishing Division
Our Sunday Visitor, Inc.
200 Noll Plaza
Huntington, Indiana 46750